PREHISTORIC TIMES

Dragon Books
Granada Publishing
8 Grafton Street, London W1X 3LA

Published by Dragon Books 1984

Copyright © Hachette 1979
This edition copyright © Granada Publishing 1984
British Library Cataloguing in Publication Data
Nougier, Louis-René
  Prehistoric times. – (Everyday lives)
  1. Man, Prehistoric – Juvenile literature
  I. Title   II. Les temps préhistoriques.
  English
  930.1   GN744

ISBN 0-583-30677-2

Printed and bound in Spain by
Graficas Reunidas, Madrid

EVERYDAY LIVES

PREHISTORIC TIMES

By Louis-René Nougier
Illustrated by Pierre Joubert

DRAGON BOOKS
Granada Publishing

CONTENTS

THE STORY OF PREHISTORIC MAN

History books used to begin with the famous phrase, 'When Julius Caesar invaded Britain . . .' This gave us a history of two thousand years which covered the deeds, joys, sufferings and hopes of sixty generations, beginning with wooden huts and war chariots and ending with today's skyscrapers and supersonic aircraft. But there was a huge period of history before this.

Fifty years ago your father probably hadn't been born. If we multiply that figure by ten and look back five hundred years, Columbus was just discovering America. Five thousand years ago peasants, shepherds, miners and workmen lived in many of the same places that we live in now. Their jobs, their houses and their ways of life were not so very different from those of people in the last century. Fifty thousand years ago our ancestors, very distant but already definitely human, hunted cave bears in a climate colder than our fiercest winters. Britain itself was uninhabited and covered in ice.

Five hundred thousand years ago (we are multiplying the years by ten each time), an older ancestor of man, called *Homo erectus* because he walked quite upright, learned to use fire. And five million years ago *Homo habilis*, a still more distant ancestor, lived on raw roots which he dug up with a stick. On his lucky days he shared a carcase with the hyenas. A little time before that, *Australopithecus* inhabited the earth. He had no weapons or tools at all, except possibly a stone, crudely shaped by being knocked against another stone. That was the sound which first announced mankind, the sound of one stone clicking against another to make a tool.

Can we possibly imagine the vast period of time – five million years – over which human beings evolved? The earth itself was formed more than five thousand million years ago, so if we use one year to represent the earth's life, our ancient ancestors would not have appeared until the last day, 31 December. Man discovered fire at about 10.00 pm and it was 11.54 pm when he started hunting cave bears. In the course of the very last minute he developed marvellous animal art and became a herdsman and farmer. Ancient Britons appeared only 46 seconds before the year's end.

History begins for Britain and western Europe in the days of the ancient Britons. The daily life of all our distant ancestors before they learned to write (prehistory) is known only from the archaeological record. We have found flints and other stones shaped for using as tools or weapons, everyday objects made of bone, kitchen rubbish dumps and traces of huts, the remains of animals our ancestors ate, and even grains of pollen from plants they collected and, much later, cultivated. We have also found fossilized parts of their skeletons, from which we can sometimes tell how long individuals lived or what illnesses they suffered from. Archaeology has interpreted this evidence and, while there are still some missing links, we now know the broad outline of the story of man.

From apes to archaeologists

During the millions of years in which man's physique evolved from that of the great apes, his way of life obviously also changed. Our ancestors ate, dressed, thought and behaved differently from us. At what point did they stop being apes and start to be human? It is difficult to say, but it is probably best to begin with some hairy characters called Australopithecines (southern apes), who existed in Africa from at least five million years ago until about one million years ago. They crouched when they walked, just like their close cousin *Homo habilis* (skilful man) who made the very first tools from pebbles. These creatures already lived in round huts made from branches and went hunting for their food.

Their successors can be called the first true men: they had brains which could be as large as those of modern man, walked quite upright, and it was they who first learned to use fire. Fossils of these men have been found right across the Old World. They were initially given different names by the scientists who identified them: *Erectus* from East Africa, *Pithecan-thropus* (ape-man) from Indonesia, *Sinanthropus* from China (Peking man), *Atlanthropus* from North Africa and Mauer Man from western Europe. All of these are now generally known by one species name, *Homo erectus* – the upright man.

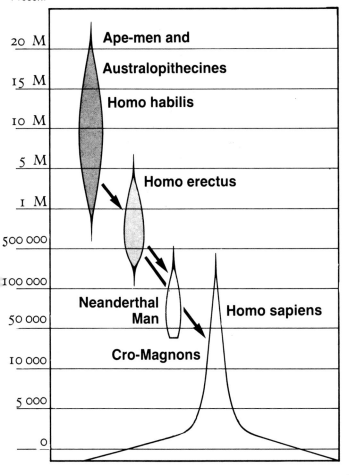

THE RISE OF MAN

Years
Before
Present

20 M — Ape-men and

15 M — Australopithecines

Homo habilis

10 M

5 M

1 M — Homo erectus

500 000

100 000

Neutanderthal
Man

50 000 — Homo sapiens

Cro-Magnons

10 000

5 000

0

Homo erectus was followed by the bigger-brained, resourceful Neanderthals, named after a little valley in the German Rhineland where their remains were first discovered in 1856, in a cave. This was the first time a human fossil had ever been found, and for a long time scientists argued about whether it really was human. Neanderthal men buried their dead with offerings, tools and wild flowers; they created better, lighter tools with points and scraping edges, with which to hunt and cut up their prey. Eighty thousand years ago there were Neanderthals spread right across the Old World, but they were not destined to survive to the present.

About forty thousand years ago Neanderthal man died out, and his place was taken by another descendant of *Homo erectus*, who perhaps adapted better than the Neanderthals to his environment. The remains of these men were first discovered in France in a rocky outcrop called Cro-Magnon, after which they were named. The Cro-Magnons and other closely related fossil men such as Chancelade and Grimaldi were *Homo sapiens* (intelligent man) like us.

It is amazing what they could do even then. The full story must wait until later chapters in the book, but here are some examples: they went hunting with such weapons as javelins, harpoons and bows; twenty thousand years ago they invented the needle; they carved wood and modelled clay; and they painted and drew bison and mammoths on the walls of caves where they lived, penetrating hundreds of metres, even kilometres deep into underground caves by the light of oil lamps. Not only were the Cro-Magnons better adapted to their environment than their forebears; they began to adapt their environment to themselves.

Five thousand years ago their descendants began, for the very first time, to produce their own food. Like us, they raised domestic animals and harvested grain crops. Soon they could produce a food surplus large enough to support members of the community engaged full-time in cultural activities – priests, administrators and ultimately . . . archaeologists.

Increase in brain size	cubic centimetres
Gibbon	90
Chimpanzee	400
Gorilla	500
Australopithecus	500–800
Homo erectus	750–1225
Neanderthal man	1450
Cro-Magnon	1590
Modern man	1000–2000

How long does it take to cut up a hyena?
Francis Poplin carved up a hyena weighing
about 60 kilograms with a rough flint
knife to see how long it would take a
prehistoric man. These are his results:

- ★ slitting the skin
  from chin to tail .... 5 minutes
- ★ skinning it to remove
  the hide whole .... 10 minutes
- ★ removing the guts and
  cutting up the carcase
  into pieces for roasting ...... 30 minutes

Total time: approximately 45 minutes
In September 1977 Richard Leakey cut up
an antelope in the same time, with the help
of a Masai herdsman, in Tanzania.
Prehistoric man could probably do it even
faster, through constant practice.

The archaeologists arrive

The pioneering work of prehistoric archaeology was begun in the nineteenth century. Since then millions of stone tools, bones and other rarer relics of prehistoric man have been found. To make sense of all this information, prehistorians have had to classify it, giving names to periods of time and to the objects found.

Prehistorians give the name *Archaic Palaeolithic* or Old Stone Age to the period in which the very earliest cultures made shaped stone tools. Nearer to our own time is the *Lower Palaeolithic* with almond-shaped tools. The *Middle Palaeolithic* sees the development of flint flake tools, good for piercing and scraping. Next comes the *Upper Palaeolithic*, when men made smaller, more efficient and diverse tools of thinner flint flakes and of bone. The remains of more recent cultures are better preserved but also more complex, with many different cultures.

The *Neolithic* or New Stone Age saw a revolution in all areas. Herdsmen and peasants introduced stock-breeding and agriculture. Workmen became more and more specialized. Merchants and seamen appeared, builders set up menhirs and dolmens, and began building Stonehenge. Four thousand years ago these new men had already mastered metal – copper and bronze first, and then iron. With the invention of writing in the Near East we reach the dawn of modern history.

The story of man need not be told in terms as dry and dull as the archaeological labels. This book highlights features of prehistoric life that mean something to us today. A pebble tool was used 1.75 million years ago in Africa in the same way as you yourself might use a similar one today to crack open a nut. When an early hunter invented the oil lamp, he created an appliance which was in constant use until the last century, and is still to be found in some households. It was not always to be made of stone, but of pottery, bronze or iron; but its shape remained the same. The needle too has lasted for twenty thousand years. The materials change but the shape stays the same and becomes part of man's everyday life.

When climatic changes or new ideas created a new way of life, the old way was never completely abandoned. Men became hunters instead of gatherers; but they still gathered berries and nuts. Indeed, even today in some of the poorer countries of the world or in times of famine, people live in the same way their prehistoric ancestors did, so it is not too difficult for us to imagine living in prehistoric times.

A CAVE OF TREASURES

An inventory of carvings and drawings in the cave of Rouffignac, in the Dordogne region of France.

150 mammoths
 26 bison
 14 goats
 12 rhinoceroses
 12 ibex
  6 snakes
  2 cats
  1 saiga antelope
  1 deer
  1 bear

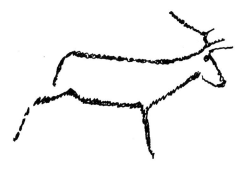

In the shadows of huge smouldering volcanoes on the Serengeti plain in east Africa, some of our ancestors (*Homo habilis*) are using stones to kill their dinner.

THE FIRST TOOL

Imagine that you are following a winding footpath through an autumn wood. Red and black blazes on the trees mark out the path so you cannot get lost in the forest. You are cheerful and safe. Nonetheless there are a few niggling problems. A nail in your shoe is hurting, there are hazelnuts under that tree, obviously ripe, but how are you going to crack them? A rivet in your rucksack has also come loose and threatens to come out altogether.

You can manage though. You look around and find a stone as big as an orange. Now you have the hammer you need: a few short accurate knocks (minding your fingers) and the nail is flattened, the nut cracked and the rivet closed. You have just used the same kind of tool as your ancient ancestors.

Scientists, archaeologists and anthropologists frequently discuss and often argue about the precise moment at which we can call our ancestors men rather than apes. Was it when they started using tools? This was certainly a watershed, though it does not by any means make man unique – chimpanzees have been known to hurl stones when threatened, and other animals, particularly some birds, use tools to help gather food. Our ancestors who started to use tools became *Homo habilis* or *Homo faber*, the maker. The first tool, like the one we imagined using just now, was probably a rough stone picked up at random, maybe as long as five million years ago. The stone would have proved useful for all sorts of jobs: shaping another stone or a piece of wood, cracking a nut, breaking open a shellfish. All human technology 22 stems from this first use of a tool.

Homo habilis was only 1.4 metres tall, so the rocks he found lying around might easily have been too heavy for him to throw. He learned to break them, and found that some freshly broken rocks had a useful cutting edge.

Australopithecines and *Homo habilis* used stones for everything: to defend themselves, to hunt, or to break open coconuts gathered on the beach so that the children could drink their milk.

23

Food for weeks: a tribe of *Homo habilis* use flints to cut the
flesh from a dead dinotherium.

The Indian Ocean washes up tasty shellfish on its shore, and sometimes even huge sperm-whales. Australopithecines are using shells to carve up a stranded whale.

Man and beast lived close to one another, sharing the same habitat and the same resources. When it came to disputes, man tended to win – his tools became deadly weapons.

SHAPING STONES

Hundreds of thousands of years passed before the rough piece of rock became a deliberately shaped tool. It took this long because the earliest people – *Australopithecus, Homo habilis* and *Homo erectus* – were scattered across the globe. The few tribes that existed were separated by immense distances, and life was dangerous and short. New ways to improve hunting or to work a piece of flint more skilfully spread very slowly, and the same techniques must have been reinvented again and again. Studying the distant past shows us just how important language and education are, as they enable us to learn things from other people's experience more quickly than we ever could do by our own trial and error.

Step by step, our prehistoric ancestors improved their flint stone pebbles until they arrived at a flat, elegant, delicately worked tool, with an aerodynamically efficient almond shape. *Homo erectus* took pleasure in its elegant shape. The workman had now become an artist.

The pictures in this chapter tell the story of a hippopotamus hunt by a tribe of *Homo erectus*. The sweeping rains have flooded Olduvai Gorge in east Africa, and *Homo erectus* is getting ready for the hunt. First he gathers and shapes his weapons from heavy stones. He has split this one so that it will fit in his hand, and now he is considering how to shape it into an axe.

Repeated, skilfully directed blows shape a lump of flint into a large, almond-shaped hand axe (above). This common tool was good for striking, crushing and scraping. The flint is first hewn roughly into shape with another stone, then carefully finished off with a piece of bone. Two boys look and learn as the craftsman makes a new hand axe (right top).

The marsh attracts both man and beast. Each evening the big mammals come to drink. The men are well aware of this and lie in wait. When a big hippopotamus appears they chase it into the marsh by shouting and waving firebrands and long spears.

The heavy animal plunges straight in and gets bogged down in the mud. The men approach carefully, stabbing the animal with their long spears wherever they can, but keeping well away from his long tusks which will become good weapons in their own turn later on!

The dead hippo has been dragged to firmer ground, where the hunters carve the animal up with their hand axes. Some cut slices of meat, others carry it off to be roasted over a hastily built fire. The tribe will be able to live for weeks off this meat – all 3000 kilograms of it!

Lightning has set fire to the forest. All the animals and men flee in terror. The men (a tribe of Homo erectus) look back in puzzlement as well as fear.

FIRE FROM HEAVEN

In 1924 Raymond Dart discovered the first *Australopithecus* fossil in a quarry in the southern African state of Botswana. In 1947 he found further pieces of skeleton at Makapansgat in the Transvaal. The bones were blackened at the ends, and the question arose: could they have been blackened by fire? A fire made two or three million years ago?

It was not so. The bones had not been blackened by fire, but by iron oxides. Our forebears probably did not master fire until half a million years later, after the days of *Australopithecus*. But how fire was discovered,

The fire has passed and burnt out. The women and children of the tribe find the burnt corpse of an antelope: pieces of meat come off easily even without a flint, and it has a new flavour. Meanwhile some of the men are courageously handling firebrands.

used, made again and preserved is difficult to discern.

Direct archaeological evidence is rare; Neanderthal-built hearths of carefully arranged stones have been found, and occasional bone ash and broken flints crazed by the heat, though these date from long after the discovery of fire by *Homo erectus*. Currently, the oldest hearths are those made half a million years ago at Vertesszolos in Hungary. We know when they were made because a skull bone from *Homo erectus* has been found among worked pebbles.

Man's earliest encounter with fire can only be imagined. The first fire was without doubt the work of nature, caused by a volcano or lightning. It must have been terrifying, but it had to be approached and tamed to be made useful – a great feat. Without it the primitive men in Europe would have frozen to death during the Ice Ages.

Normally everyone flees in terror from the lava that pours out of a volcano. One day a brave man lights a branch in this river of fire; he is about to make fire a useful ally instead of an enemy.

The wooded savannah burns in the distance after a lightning strike. The tribe rush out of their huts to watch the spectacle.

Man soon learned that fire needs to be fed with wood to stay alive, just as he needed to be fed with meat or fruit.

THE CONQUEST OF FIRE

Just as their ability to shape tools marked early humans as different from the animals whose environment they shared, so their ability to master natural forces and use them for their own benefit enabled them to dominate their world.

It is at least half a million years now since men tamed fire. Born of lightning and lava flows, fire was fierce and wild but human beings got the better of it and captured it. It was probably the women who became its guardians, staying awake to keep this hot glowing morsel of the sun alive.

At dawn or dusk, a calm peace lies on this little village of small, round huts, just like the Masai tribe's *manyata*. The night watchman tends the fires which surround and protect the village.

You had to stay alert on the savannah, even at night.
Animals came down to waterholes to drink, hyenas prowled
and the big cats went hunting, gliding through the rustling
grass. Men learned to chase them off with firebrands.

Fire could be used for roasting, but it could also be used to
make better weapons. The man on the right, who is 35 or 40

years old (a ripe old age for many *Homo erectus*), is using fire to harden the point of his spear.

Neanderthal man (above) survived the savage climate of the Ice Age in deep, dark caves, thanks to his control of fire. But he was not the only animal to seek shelter in caves. In front of a cliff full of potential homes, Neanderthal men plan their hunt; very probably they used some sort of language. The long lances are ready, the torches are lit and the men move off.

Around the fire the tribe gathered and learned from it. Its flames could make a piece of wood as hard as rock, so a branch could become a tough boar spear. Clay hardened and some stones (metal ore) changed form when they were heated. The fire's flames terrified animals, small and large, and kept the humans safe from wolves and tigers. Mysterious and terrible, fire had provoked panic and aroused awe in man for thousands of years. Now fire became an ally under man's control. It could be produced at will and put to use – as a weapon or a means of defence.

For Neanderthal man the hearth was a social centre. With it came other human ways: religious ritual, the burial of the dead. Gradually, with the help of fire, man was becoming more human.

This desirable residence (below) already has occupants; a large bear and her cubs. But blinded by the torch and pierced by fire-hardened lances which allow her tormentors to stay out of reach of her claws, the big bear falls.

MAN, THE HUNTER

This elephant has been chased into a bog and has got stuck. A tribe of little *Homo erectus* attack it with spears; the elephant gores one with his tusks, but he is trapped and outnumbered.

FOOD FOR THE TAKING

Before man discovered tools and fire, he still had to eat. For thousands of years, man-like apes living alongside animals fed in the same way. A few years ago Mary Leakey, the anthropologist, working at Laetolil in Tanzania, found, in volcanic ash that was 3.5 million years old, the footprints of an Australopithecine alongside those of prehistoric antelopes and a dinotherium, an ancestor of the elephants. This pre-man who lived with the beasts was not entirely without tools. He used the limbs with which nature had equipped him to help gather whatever nature offered – just like other animals. The dinotherium unearthed roots with its long curved tusks; the early man used his hands. Maybe he even kept stores of food like a wood mouse. There were wild fruits to gather, shellfish to collect on the seashore, and carrion to share with hyenas and vultures. Certainly with so few men in a land rich in vegetation and teeming with animals, there was no shortage of food.

Primitive humans gathered fruits, berries, runners and roots for food. These women have noticed some little rodents running away, their mouths stuffed full of roots to store in their burrows for winter. Using a sharpened stick as a digging tool, the humans open up the burrows to steal their stores.

Wild corn was harvested increasingly from 5000 B.C. Sheaves were cut with a sickle made from a curved piece of wood with flint teeth stuck into it; then the ears were threshed on a wattle – a wicker frame – to extract the grain.

These men (above) are breaking off limpets with a quartz pick on the Atlantic coast of northern Spain (around 6000 B.C.). The seaside must have provided a lot of resources for early man, but because coastlines change a great deal there is very little archaeological evidence to be found there.

Recently a study has been made of the bushmen who live on the edge of the Kalahari desert. In nineteen days they collected enough food to live on for a hundred days! There was no chance of them going hungry. Their regular diet gives them 2400 calories a day; a middle-aged, medium-sized western European adult eats only 2200 calories.

Each region has its own natural resources. Around 3000 B.C., people living around the Baltic Sea found pieces of gleaming amber on their beaches and used them to make beads for necklaces. Other people living hundreds of kilometres further south in the Carpathian mountains had plenty of rock salt, and brought great lumps of it down the river Vistula (through present-day Poland) in canoes. The girl on the left is trading amber she has collected for rock salt, which her herd animals need.

Around 7000 B.C. men lived in the Danish marshes of Maglemose on timber platforms, in wigwams covered in birch bark. They lived by fishing and collecting shellfish. 51

HUNTING WITH CUNNING

On the edge of the forest *Australopithecus* and *Homo habilis* would have come across the tracks and maybe carcases of the larger wild animals that lived on the grassy plains of the savannah. When they acquired a taste for meat as well as plant food, they would have had to learn how to kill instead of just collecting their food or eating carrion.

Living so close to nature, the early hunters would have known that certain places were better than others for catching their prey. Animals, like men, had accidents. Instead of being killed they might be immobilized and need only to be finished off. At two Spanish prehistoric sites – Torralba and Ambrona –

A mysterious painting in Combarelles (southern France) may represent a scene like this. Some Cro-Magnon men are driving a herd of wild reindeer into pits filled with spiked stakes.

As twilight falls the Neanderthals hear an angry bellow.
They rush out with torches and spears. A woolly rhino en
route to its watering hole has fallen into their trap.

These Neanderthals are digging a pit with a bison's shoulder blade. It is a difficult task, especially since the soil is still partly frozen. They will set up pointed stakes in the pit, and disguise it with branches: the trap is ready.

there is evidence that on their way to drink, elephants sometimes got stuck in the mud of the marshes. As these great mammals weighed five tonnes they had no chance of getting out. So with shouts, blazing torches and long spears the hunters chased the terrified creatures further into the soggy ground.

Animals would also sometimes fall down cliffs and break their limbs, or tumble into pits. In one natural hole under a cave in France lie the remains of a great bison, a reindeer, a wolf, foxes, young bears, a panther and a wolverine. All fell into the deep hole and were unable to escape. Man learned to copy these natural traps. Hunting with traps preceded pursuit, and already required a cooperative effort. To dig a pit and drive an animal into it took several people working together; a man alone would never have survived.

Attach some stones to rawhide thongs and you have a bolas.
This weapon is used to fell an animal by entangling its limbs.

These Magdalenian hunters (around 10,000 B.C.) have
trapped a ptarmigan lured by food on the snowy ground; the
bird's wings have stuck to the stakes which are coated with
sticky resin.

Weighing 6 to 10 tonnes was no use if you got stuck in the mud – a big mammoth (above) simply couldn't struggle out. These Cro-Magnon hunters (and the wolves) are waiting at a respectful distance until the mammoth is exhausted. Then they will close in for the kill.

These Neanderthals are camouflaging themselves before setting out on a major hunting expedition. They wash in the river and rub red ochre over their bodies, so that they can creep nearer to their prey without being seen.

57

Unwittingly helping man, a pack of wolves has driven a herd of reindeer right past the hunters' hide. The men (Cro-Magnons) rush
58 out, bow in hand, to shoot their prey.

HUNTING GAME

In Europe the reindeer was the mainstay of the Stone Age hunters. Each beast weighed 200 kilograms and gave 100 kilograms of juicy meat. The Magdalenians – a people who lived in France between 16,000 and 10,000 B.C. – used the bones and antlers to make weapons and tools, the skin for tents and clothes, and the tendons and nerves to make thread. Even today the Lapps retain a similar reindeer culture.

Reindeer lived in herds of several hundred and were easy to hunt since there were far more reindeer than men. The entire population of western Europe during the Stone Age was probably less than 100,000 people. Pictures of reindeer were frequently carved on tools, though strangely they were rarely depicted on cave walls. Perhaps, explained Abbé Breuil, the

The animals are gutted, weighted with heavy stones, and then hung in the fast, icy waters of a glacier stream where they will keep for a whole season: the first refrigerator!

There's a use to be found for every bit of a reindeer. The
chief cuts up the meat and sets aside the antlers and bones for
making tools, needles and weapons. In front of their hunting

shelter two women prepare the guts for use as ropes. The
boy in the foreground will get twenty metres of thong out
of his two square metres of hide, by cutting it in a spiral.

61

At night, the hunters cut up and cook the reindeer they have killed. Some meat is roasted and eaten immediately, some will be smoked over a green wood fire. Some pieces are thrown to the wolves more to keep them at bay than as a reward for their part in the day's hunting.

archaeologist, reindeer were too common and too easy to catch for it to be thought necessary to use magic in hunting them.

On the other hand, bison were frequently drawn by the Magdalenians. A third of all the pictures which have been found are of bison, making these almost as common as pictures of horses. Perhaps the hunter desired the speed of the horse and the strength of the bison. The bison, weighing up to 1500 kilograms, was a common and useful animal. As well as its delicious flesh, if killed in the autumn it also supplied masses of fat which was stored in its hump – its reserves for the coming winter.

COMPLEAT ANGLERS

The aim of both hunting and fishing was to kill animals to eat. Fast-moving animals, such as reindeer or salmon, were difficult to catch, and for thousands of years the same weapons were used for hunting both types of creature: javelins, bone-pointed spears with flint heads fastened to wood or reed shafts, and harpoons. It was not until Magdalenian times that specialized fishing weapons and tackle appeared: splinters of bone carefully bent and sharpened into fish-hooks. These men also started to use two-pronged harpoons and barbed javelins for fishing.

The riverside inhabitants of Maglemose in Denmark, who lived about eight thousand years ago,

These Cro-Magnons are fishing with their bare hands, tickling trout. Sometimes they made necklaces out of a trout's small vertebrae (backbone segments).

used all kinds of wood but mostly hazel to make eel-pots, dams and fish traps, which have been perfectly preserved in the marsh peat. When fishing nets were invented a little later, man had a complete fishing arsenal identical to that which we use today. The shapes remain the same even though the materials are quite different – we have iron traps instead of osier ones, and we use steel for hooks instead of bone.

Fishing techniques, then, have not changed very much, unlike hunting techniques which changed constantly, becoming faster and more warlike.

These Cro-Magnon fishermen (right) lived in caves in the steep cliffs of Pindal bay in northern Spain. They used to spear a kind of tunny fish with three-pronged harpoons.

This boy, from a lakeside village in the Alps, is inspecting his fishing line. He uses a notched stone for a weight, and pieces of bark for floats; the hooks (which are not barbed) are made of bone.

A series of wattle gates seals off this stream (above), so that fish trapped between them can easily be caught by hand. When the rivers were too deep or wide for gates, men trapped fish in eelpots (right top) made of willow twigs (osier).

Around 8000 B.C. these fisherfolk (below) set up their 'smoking factory' under a rocky overhang. Trout were slit open, gutted and filleted. The fillets were laid on hurdles over a slow fire of oak or beech charcoal, which was kept damp so that it gave off a lot of smoke. The smoked fish would last up to a whole season.

Winter is coming. It is time to dig a pit-dwelling for the winter, with a good roof of timber, branches and earth to keep out the foul weather.

LIVING IN CAVES

Every man needs a roof over his head – and nearly always has done. Prehistoric men sought shelter from excessive heat and cold, from chill winds, from the violence of tropical thunderstorms or the persistent drizzle of the western seaboard.

A cave was the most efficient natural shelter they could find – caves not only keep out the wind and the rain, they also maintain a constant temperature of about ten to fifteen degrees centigrade. A cave is cool in very hot weather and mild in fierce frosts. Unfortunately caves are rare and only to be found in limestone regions where water has dissolved the rock, leaving natural caverns. Wookey Hole in Somerset seems to have been used as a summer residence by prehistoric hunters.

A tribe of Australopithecines are out hunting on the vast
open savannah with no shelter except the occasional isolated
copse of trees. A thunderstorm is on its way so the women
quickly build a shelter to protect their children. After
sticking some broken branches into the ground, they weave
twigs and branches between them to make a windbreak. In
the background you can see a finished hut. Thousands of
years later, bushmen in the Kalahari Desert still build similar
shelters when out hunting.

Caves were sometimes improved by adding wind-
breaks or stone walls. Men also created artificial
caves, in other words, huts and houses. Excavations
at Olduvai (Tanzania) have revealed a circle of large
stones, believed to be the base of a hut that was built a
million years ago. Some dwellings were dug out of
the ground to give better protection from the wind
and to take advantage of the ground's warmth.
Hunters in Siberia and in the Ukraine had such
pit-dwellings.

A Neanderthal man is bringing his rather meagre pickings home. Home is a shelter of tree trunks held in place by stones and covered with branches, under a rocky overhang.

Hunters sometimes had to leave their houses: a herd of reindeer might pass and an expedition would set out to follow them over great distances. Unless they found shelter in caves or natural overhangs on their route, they would erect skin tents as temporary shelters.

A blizzard is blowing. For months and months the plain will be covered in deep snow. A wolf pack is racing across the plain, desperate for food, as the Magdalenian hunters come home to a warm and comfortable underground shelter.

This natural shelter will give little wind protection, so these Cro-Magnon men have put down their weapons to build a wall of boulders.

A hunter relaxes in his hut. In the entrance tunnel the women tend the fire. The hunter uses a delicate flint chisel to carve a piece of mammoth ivory into a figure.

Mammoth hunters use the remains of their prey to build their huts. The foundations are piles of skulls, pelvic bones and shoulder blades. The tusks make fine roof frames. On

the left, the woman is scraping a skin which will become
part of the covering.

PERMANENT HOMES

Wood and clay were the best building materials available in Neolithic times. They were easy to find, easy to work with, and kept the cold, heat and rain out.

In Mediterranean regions the forest was destroyed by fires, started either by lightning or by shepherds who wanted open pastures. This left only moors and scrublands, so there was no wood for building. In the west and north of Britain the climate did not allow trees suitable for timber to grow, so farmers on Dartmoor or in the Orkneys built stone houses (like those at Skara Brae).

They developed a building technique called 'corbelling'. For this they used limestone, which is found naturally in horizontal beds that are not too thick, and

This peasant is building a house of wattle (branches interwoven between stakes) and daub (mud).

A village of beehive huts in Ireland; you can see how they got their name. It's a shepherds' village, and there are sheepskins drying on the nearest hut.

Hold your breath! These men are placing the keystone on a vaulted hut built of limestone blocks. When they remove the props, will it stay up?

These forest peasants have built their village of circular huts where two rivers meet. It is an excellent spot, easy to defend against men or beasts, near their fields and close enough to the forest for wood and game. They can fish from their doorsteps!

cleaves naturally into regular blocks. The builder piles these blocks one on top of another, each stone slightly overhanging the one below it, so that the tops of the walls meet over the middle of the building. The blocks are not laid entirely flat, but with a slight inclination to the outside so that the rain will run off them. This technique was used to build the 'beehive' huts of western Ireland, the trulli of Italy and the monumental Maes Howe in Orkney. These huts were only prevented from falling down by the weight of the walls leaning against each other, and from time to time they did fall down, but they were easily put together again. The oldest ones we know are nearly six thousand years old.

78

There are no trees in the Orkneys, so the fishing and farming
people of Skara Brae (about 1500 B.C.) built their houses of
stone, and below ground level for wind protection.
Everything is made of stone: beds, cupboards, shelves and
hearth.

ART AND MAGIC

These Cro-Magnon hunters, painted with ochre and dressed in animal skins, are performing an awe-inspiring dance in front of their tribe.

HUNTERS' MAGIC

Prehistoric huntsmen drew, painted or carved mammoths, bison, horses and ibex on the walls of deep caves. Obviously some of these hunters were artists who took pleasure in drawing animals, but there was originally a deeper, more important reason for their works. They were creating far more than mere drawings or paintings. The drawings represented the animals themselves by a kind of creative magic which placed them completely under the artist's power. This was the beginning of magic.

Imagine a group of hunters in their cave admiring the marvellous bison painted by the great artist of the tribe. Suddenly one of them is inspired to seize a brush, dip it into the black manganese colour and draw one, two, three arrows, mortally 'wounding' the animal. His companions cheer. The bison is dead;

Neanderthal men came across this strange-shaped rock deep inside the cave of Toirano in Liguria (northern Italy). Perhaps it seemed to them like a weird animal; at any rate for some reason they bombarded it with lumps of clay, which can still be seen today sticking to the rock.

This Magdalenian man is experimenting with stencilling, an age-old artistic technique. He presses his hand against the wall and spits ochre over it, leaving a permanent image when he takes his hand away.

their game is ready for the feast. This was a new rite: magic called the beast into the hunters' presence and enabled them to 'kill' it, thus assuring the hunters of success – and of their supply of food.

There are several mammoths on the walls of a cave at Rouffignac in France. Two are depicted coming into the cave, and two others are leaving – with a calf. Their young mammoth was 'born' in the cave. Here was another magical rite, which must have given reassurance to the hunters that there would continue to be enough mammoths to eat.

In front of the carvings of animals in some sites, there are walkways like viewing platforms. Discussions, songs and dances, even the first religious or magical 'theatre', could well have taken place there. 83

Some of the huntsmen who used the cave of Gargas had
84 horribly mutilated hands: many of their finger-joints had

fallen off as a result of appalling chilblains. The witchdoctor
spat ochre on to their hands to help them heal.

MEDICINAL MUD

Medicine and surgery began long before the time of the Greek doctor Hippocrates (fifth to fourth centuries B.C.) whom we call the 'father of medicine'. Man seems to have been aware of the healing powers of mud and ochre for about thirty thousand years. Mud contains micro-organisms which might soothe or help to heal, and even today some doctors recommend mud-baths to their patients. Mud can also preserve corpses. Tombs have been found that were coated with a mixture of mud and red ochre, probably applied to preserve the remains of the deceased. A famous example is the 'red lady of Paviland', a skeleton (male but originally supposed to be female) found in a cave in Pembroke, which had been covered in ochre twenty-eight thousand years ago. There are also prints of hands crippled by chilblains and treated with ochre on the walls of a cave in
France.

An elder of the tribe takes a heated flint from the fire, and inscribes a letter 'T' with it in this girl's skull. She will be marked for life – the mark is still visible on some skulls (mostly female ones) that have been found in recent times. Why it was done – to cure some ailment, as an initiation rite, as a punishment? – nobody knows.

In a cave in Oran in north Africa, lived a witchdoctor who used to knock out two of his patients' top teeth with a flint chisel. Perhaps they thought it improved their looks?

Operations called trepanations, in which the skull is opened up, were first performed nearly five thousand years ago and were often successful. There is a skull in the institute of Anthropology at Cluj (Romania) which had been trepanned, presumably to cure a tumour on the brain. The patient clearly survived, because the wound (a small hole) healed over, but the abscess must have come back since a second trepanation was performed right next to the first. The patient survived again!

This surgeon is cutting out a circle of bone, like the one he's wearing as a pendant, from the centre of his patient's skull – perhaps to let out evil spirits. If the sick man survived the operation (known now as trepanning) his wound would heal.

These Neanderthals' chief has died of old age – at forty. Using a bison's shoulder blade to dig a grave, his companions bury him with his weapons so that he can hunt in the next world. This is the first evidence of religious belief. A heavy stone was put over the grave to keep the hyenas out.

THE ARTISTS ARRIVE

Have you ever scribbled a jumble of lines on a blank piece of paper out of boredom, and then found that you could recognize a mountain or an animal in the doodle? Well, that probably first happened thirty thousand years ago. Perhaps a bison hunter trailed his fingers through the damp clay of a cave, and produced the likeness of something he recognized – a bison's hump. He drew some more lines for the body and four vertical strokes for the legs. He had made a bison!

The bison hunters are getting ready for the chase. The chiefs puts three handprints over one of the bison drawings, perhaps as a magic gesture to enable the hunters to kill three bisons? The earliest drawings were certainly part of a hunting magic, though no doubt artists took pleasure in a good picture for its own sake too.

A thousand metres inside the cave, the artist (above) is
carving a mammoth in hard limestone. Abbé Breuil
nicknamed this animal the 'cheeky mammoth', because of
the way it looks at you.

Perhaps, again, the shape of a natural lump of rock reminded a hunter of some animal. A few more lines, carved or painted on to the rock, reinforced the resemblance. The other hunters came to see this strange image, this magic. And if, soon afterwards, they captured a beast which they had drawn, they might well have thought that making the picture had put it in their power.

Today, some people are good at drawing and some not. It must have been the same even ten or twenty thousand years ago. Perhaps even, one man in a tribe who was especially good at drawing bison might spend all day painting friezes while the others went out to hunt. In the evenings the others would bring a haunch of venison or a bison's brain to the artist as payment.

The most spectacular of these cave paintings that have survived are at Lascaux, Rouffignac and Niaux in France, and at Altamira in Spain.

Long ago on the Danube plain near Vienna, fishermen return home with their catch. The village artist will be given a share for carving a small piece of ivory into the famous Willendorf figurine.

These huntsmen discover that they can make patterns by drawing their fingers across wet clay on the walls of a cave. Perhaps this is how cave paintings began.

With a wad of fur, the artist draws does made out of dots of paint. The ground is represented by a crack in the rock.

An artist's studio! While his assistants hold the long torches of juniper wood, feed the oil lamps or mix colours, the Grand Master of Rouffignac draws a frieze of mammoths.

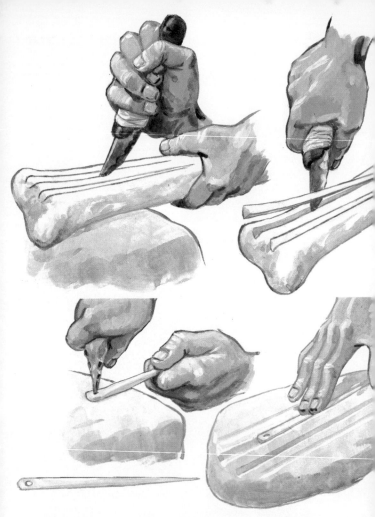

How do you make a needle? Take a large bone, and cut long, straight grooves in it with a knife or chisel. Using a sharp knife, cut out a splinter of bone. One end needs to be sharpened, and the other levelled off before being perforated with an awl. You can polish the finished product on a piece of sandstone.

SKINS AND NEEDLES

It may be hard for a camel to get through the eye of a needle, but before 16,000 B.C. it was certainly impossible! Seldom can such a small invention have had such great consequences. The needle gradually transformed the daily life of man, and it led to a host of new inventions. Before the needle, people wore plain skins thrown over the shoulder or wrapped around the waist; now they could sew them together to make garments shaped to the wearer's body. A drawing of an anorak with a hood can be seen in the cave of Gabillou – the world's first fashion picture.

Nowadays we make needles from steel. The material has changed but the tool that we have inherited is the same.

Holes were made, in the same way as for needles, in decorations for necklaces and pendants, such as animal teeth, shells and pieces of bone. What better talisman for the huntsman, than a necklace of his prey's teeth!

These hunter-fishermen are covering a frame of wood or whale bones with sewn hides to make a light, portable boat. Even today, Irish fishermen in the Aran Islands and Welsh river fishermen use similar boats (currachs and coracles), though they now use tarred canvas rather than skins.

People also made leather waterbags by sewing several skins together. If you filled one with water and threw in stones from the fire, it was possible to boil the water for cooking. Sewn waterbags above all made early man more mobile: he could carry water in them on long journeys, or alternatively he could fill them with air and use them as floats for swimming long distances.

After the waterbag came the kayak. Animal hides were stretched and sewn on to a skeleton structure of wood or long bones. The Eskimos still use the kayak. Men put their provisions for a journey in other leather bags which they stored in the boat, so that 98 their food was kept safe, waterproof and unsinkable.

A rough tripod supports a leaky waterbag. The woman puts
hot stones in to heat the water for a delicious reindeer soup.

These women are sewing hides, specially treated to make
them supple, into fitted clothes. They use thin rawhide, gut,
or tendons (made supple by chewing) as threads. The

huntsmen are using rawhide ropes to drag a horse they have
killed towards their hut.

SETTLING DOWN

Once their fire has destroyed a patch of forest, the men move in. They chop tree trunks into pointed stakes and fix them in the ground to make walls for their cabins.

THE FORESTS RISE AND FALL

When the Ice Age came to an end, ten thousand years ago, the climate became milder and wetter. Only the far north was still tundra, and man could live in Britain again. The pine and birch trees of the marshy taiga between a line from Oslo to Leningrad and a line from Bordeaux to Belgrade, gave way to a huge leafy forest of elms, oaks and lime – the 'mixed oak wood' which stretched from the Urals to England. This forest was full of game such as deer and wild boar.

The first settlers felled timber to create clearings for their crops. They had invented a new tool, the paring-knife, whose grooved edge was ideal for woodwork. They also used picks and axes with heads made of large pieces of flint.

The settlers lived in villages of round huts with conical roofs. Log fences prevented wild boar from

This forester is cutting out a drinking or eating trough for his animals with his adze. All the farm's equipment is made of wood. The sheep have salt to lick from a wooden bowl.

The farmer's plough was made of three big pieces of wood, and drawn with a yoke by a pair of oxen. The blade, a large shaped flint, turned the soil. Straight furrows made sowing and harvesting much easier.

Foresters used to capture young wild boars and pen them with their own domestic pigs. The half-wild piglets improved the breed and produced tastier meat.

trampling over the cultivated plots, and kept the livestock – pigs and cattle – safely enclosed. The dog, which was domesticated about ten thousand years ago, now became an invaluable companion and aid in hunting deer or boar, guarding herds or fighting wolves.

Because they used such a wide range of natural resources, these people flourished and the population grew. They continually had to create new clearings in order to let the land recover. As they burned and cut the wood the clearings gradually joined one another and so, bit by bit, they created the great treeless plain of north Europe, across which the biting Siberian winds blow.

The boys light and stoke a fire under a tree, which will make it much easier to chop down with their flint axes (which looked very like modern steel ones). In the foreground of this picture two men are hollowing out a dugout canoe with adzes.

There were lots of animals in deciduous forests (above).
Deer (not reindeer) were common, and so the wild
boar, which was hunted for its succulent meat. This hunter
has captured a live piglet in his net. He will probably fatten
it up to eat when it is bigger.

FROM HUNTER
TO HERDSMAN

For thousands of years man was exposed to the uncertainties of hunting. He had to slaughter a mammoth, or find one dead of exhaustion or sickness, to fill his larder. A herd of reindeer, or later of red deer, would feed the tribe for several days. Any meat left over could be preserved by smoking it over a fire of green wood, but the reserves would always run out and it was soon time to look for the next herd.

The first domestic flocks and herds probably began with individual animals – a young wild sheep may have been captured alive and kept, or perhaps a lamb whose mother had been killed was kept and raised by the men to be slaughtered when it was full grown. Perhaps a hunter kept some calves alive, or a wounded animal allowed itself to be captured and cared for; maintaining and breeding whole flocks and herds is but a short step from this. It was obviously quicker and easier to kill a captive animal when the children were hungry than to set out on a long, uncertain and perhaps dangerous hunting expedition.

Six thousand years ago, 40 per cent of the meat eaten in some parts of Europe was domestic-bred mutton, and a thousand years later it was 75 per cent. Skins and meat from their own sheep, goats and

Today this land is desert, but six thousand years ago men herded long-horned cattle at Tassili n'Ajjer in the Sahara.
108 This herdsman is painting his animals on a rock face.

(later) cattle gave prehistoric men a thoroughly reliable food supply for the first time. Hunting did not stop of course. Wild bulls, roe, red and fallow deer, boar, horses and gazelles were still tracked down in the wild. Even today people poach and hunt animals.

The domestication of animals changed the balance of nature. Grazing flocks and herds destroyed the forests, and bleak moors were formed whose unprotected soil was eroded by wind and rain.

The shepherds shear their sheep outside their great square sheepfold. The women then wash the wool in a running stream before spinning it by hand on a distaff.

A shepherd of the New Stone Age (right) and his dog – an early Alsatian – guard their flock. He has a curved crook which was already the shepherd's tool and symbol. Crooks have been found carved on rocks all round the Mediterranean.

A New Stone Age fortified village. It is encircled by a deep ditch. The inhabitants built ramparts with the soil they dug from the ditch and used the flints they found for tools. Cattle were led out of the palisaded compound to their pastures across a causeway.

A simple loom (right). Archaeologists have only recovered the weights at the bottom, which were notched pebbles or pieces of baked clay for stretching the warp (the vertical threads). The weaver passed the shuttle with the woof (the horizontal thread) in and out between these upright threads. The small patches of cloth this made were sewn together to make clothes like the dress the weaver is wearing.

113

This peasant woman is making holes in the soil with a
dibble, and planting seeds in them. In the distance, a party of
men are levelling the ground with a heavy wooden sledge
full of branches.

THE FIRST FARMERS

Thanks to the domestication of animals such as sheep or cattle, the 'hunter' had his prey ready to hand and under his control. With the beginning of agriculture, the peasant also raised grain and root crops in front of his own hut.

The discovery of crop cultivation was a major leap forward; it was a sign of man's increasing understanding of nature. In the beginning our ancestors collected wild grasses because they liked the grain – the nourishing little seeds. Then they learned to crush the grain to make a sort of flour for porridge or flat bread cakes. But it took much more intelligence for the nomadic tribesman to observe that it was these grains, buried in the soil, that produced little green shoots in spring, and after flowering produced new seeds at the end of summer.

Farmhouses were built near the fields, which had to be protected to stop sheep or wild boar from destroying the crops. Some at least of these people had to visit the fields regularly to weed them. Sowing and harvesting had to be communal activities, so the farmers' houses were built close together, forming the first farming villages.

This young woman is kneading wet clay before she starts to
116 make pots.

This girl is using a pebble to shape a lump of clay into a pot. The first pots had a round, deep shape like a waterbag. The potters must have noticed the resemblance, because they sometimes decorated them with stitch-marks.

Pottery that has simply been dried in the sun is too fragile; it has to be baked in a wood fire or an oven before it is any use. This pile of pots and firewood will be covered with soil to keep the heat (and some air) in, then set alight.

The corn is spread out on the ground and a threshing-sledge
(a heavy board with flint teeth) is dragged over it to break
the husks and release the grain. The man at the front of the
picture is knocking loose flint teeth back into a sledge.

Eight thousand years ago the Hoggar valley in the Sahara
was a fertile land with running rivers, full of elephants, rhinos
and hippos. The people who lived there around 600 B.C.
(below) were some of the first to cultivate cereals. The boy is
winnowing the threshed corn, throwing it up into the air so
that the chaff (straw and husks) is blown away and the grain
is left behind. The woman is grinding the grain into flour.

This harvester (above) cuts his corn with a sickle, a curved piece of wood inset with flint splinters. It looked very like a sheep's jawbone, which is probably why the ancient Egyptian word 'Ma' meant both 'sickle' and 'jawbone'.

THE FIRST SAILORS

Prehistoric man lived a tough life close to nature; he probably learned to swim very early on. Some anthropologists even think men used to live much of the time in water, wading along lake and sea shores to avoid predators. They may not have had the style or speed of modern athletes, but their stamina was amazing. We know that *Pithecanthropus* and Neanderthal man crossed wide stretches of water including the Straits of Gibraltar and the Bosporus.

Forest hunters and peasants would have watched logs floating in the marshes or on the sea, and no doubt used them to help stay afloat. They must soon have found out that a hollowed-out log did not roll over – they had invented the dugout canoe still used today. Where there were no trees with big enough trunks, men made light boats by binding together bunches of reeds.

As well as making waterbags, the Magdalenians sewed skins together to make buoys, and no doubt used them just as children today use plastic or rubber water-wings. In northern Europe the hunter-fisherman stretched skins over frames to make boats called coracles or currachs, like the Eskimo kayaks but oval in shape. These boats were capable of making very long journeys; in 1977 Tim Severin crossed the Atlantic in one of them!

A popular port of call on the island of Vingen in Norway. Some canoeists record their visit by carving pictures of their boats on the rock face. Perhaps they got the idea from the elk hunters who had carved pictures of elks there two or three thousand years earlier.

These fishermen are dragging a long net behind their dugout canoes. They will gut, dry and smoke some of the fish they catch to preserve them. These people lived on big platforms beside lakes in the Alps five or six thousand years ago. They hunted, fished, herded animals, grew cereals and had easy access to the forest. They were very prosperous.

This fisherman (right) uses the earliest kind of boat – a log. He lived near Maglemose on the shores of the Baltic nearly ten thousand years ago, and hunted tunny fish with his bow and arrows.

123

On the Aran Islands fishermen (right) scour the beaches for pieces of driftwood, with which they build frames for their currachs.

The women gather armfuls of long, thick reeds. The men then tie these into tight sheaves to be made into light boats. The wooden log acts as a keel. Reed boats are still used in Sardinia, on the Nile, on Lake Chad and 4000 metres up in the Andes on Lake Titicaca. Thor Heyerdahl recently sailed across the Atlantic in one!

An early flint mine. Miners dig straight down, fifteen metres or more if necessary, to the beds of flint. The roof above the mine shaft kept out sun and rain.

By the light of an oil lamp a team of miners dig a gallery deep underground. The leader pulls out flint nodules which his assistant passes back. These men had to work in an atmosphere thick with chalk dust. They probably suffered from the miners' lung disease called silicosis.

DOWN THE MINES

Mediterranean herdsmen and Danubian peasants did not use much flint; there were quite enough pebbles on the river-banks for making their axes and adzes. Forest-dwellers in Britain and north Europe on the other hand, used quantities of flint for making paring knives, axes and hoes. They had to till heavy soils and cut down trees, so the flints lying on the surface were soon used up.

Men started digging down to the layers of flint which ran through chalk beds. At Harrow Hill (Middlesex) men simply dug straight down at first, but below a certain depth these pits became dangerous. One of the first engineers had the idea of digging a large pit as deep as it could safely be made, and then

Many of the pit shafts dug five or six thousand years ago were only eighty centimetres wide. The miners climbed up and down like modern rock climbers, pressing their feet and backs against the sides of the 'chimney'. The flint was put in baskets and pulled up by rope.

Here's a fine specimen of flint, says the mine overseer to a merchant. You can see beds of flint in the chalk cliffs above the mine.

129

In Grime's Graves in Norfolk, four or five thousand years ago, pits were dug with very wide shafts, up to five metres across. They used notched tree trunks as ladders. This man fortunately does not have far to fall.

excavating horizontal tunnels radiating out from it.

These early flint miners were very choosy. They ignored poor quality flint and exploited only the best veins. At a mine in Spiennes in Belgium they quarried to a depth of fifteen metres (the height of a five-storey building). If the chalk was hard they used flint picks, but when the going was easier they used picks made from antlers. One thousand five hundred picks have been found in one pit alone!

When a gallery became dangerously long, a new shaft was dug. Four hundred flint mines have been found in groups of five at Grime's Graves in Norfolk. Abandoned pits were filled up (and thus made safe) with the debris from new ones. Some flint mines were in use for long periods – one mine in Belgium was worked for a hundred and twenty years before it was exhausted, over three thousand years ago.

The long gallery of this more advanced mine is supported with timber props, and goes straight into the mountainside. These miners are carrying out a heavy load of rock salt, which was an important trade item.

Bronze and copper were at first used only for axes and daggers. This workman is making a sandstone mould in the shape of the weapon, with a vent to let gases escape.

The metalworker takes the molten metal and pours it into the mould. Because it is being made in a two-piece mould, 132 the axe will have a burr (a rough edge) at the join.

MIXING METALS

About 2500 B.C., new metals were introduced to the West. Gold and copper had been used in Egypt for a thousand years already; they were hard and compact as they were found in the soil, and while difficult to shape into axe-heads, they could be hammered as thin as a leaf. Using metal-working technology learned from the East, smelters threw the ore into furnaces heated by wood or charcoal, and the molten metal was poured into moulds at temperatures of 1100°C. Copper axes blunted quickly, however.

Then someone discovered that copper mixed with other metals (lead in Turkey, tin in the West) formed a harder metal with a sharper cutting edge – bronze. When people discovered how to make bronze with an

Once the axe had cooled it was taken out of its mould. The blade would be sharpened on a piece of sandstone. The rough edges (burr) on the dagger are hammered smooth on an anvil.

alloy of three parts of copper to one of tin, they could make better weapons – axes, daggers and the first swords – and tools than ever before. From 700 B.C. the Halstatt culture in north Europe learned to work iron (though the Hittites in Asia Minor beat them to it by eight hundred years).

People started to prospect for minerals. Canoeists set out across the Channel to find tin in Cornwall, and settlers followed in the wake of prospectors all over Europe.

A shepherd boy stencils his bronze dagger on a red schist rockface with a quartz knife, next to the picture he has made of a horned ox's head.

Metal traders (right), loaded down with weapons and other bronze objects, are ambushed. They will probably get the better of their opponents. Bronze weapons were sharper and deadlier than flint ones, and the new weapon, the sword, was

terrifyingly effective.

A forge in Anatolia (in Turkey) at the beginning of the Bronze Age
(about four thousand years ago). These high furnaces (two metres tall)
were stoked by wood fires. The molten metal came pouring out at the
bottom.

FROM VILLAGES
TO FORTRESSES

In 5000 B.C. there were about 30 million human beings on earth. Only three thousand years later, there were 300 million people! Villages grew in size and importance, and some degree of planning became essential. This took many forms.

The new villages bristled with defences including ditches, palisades, high ramparts, watch-towers and drawbridges. They were built for extra security on hills (Maiden Castle), peninsulas (Hengistbury), or islands (Dun Aengus, Aran Isles), and one can still often see their remains. The ancient architects became strategists and they built more compact villages in order to be able to defend them more easily.

Building a village at Neuchâtel lake in Switzerland (below). A bullock cart brings clay, gravel and timber to reinforce and build up the banks. A heavy rock suspended from a gantry is used to drive timber piles deep into the lake bed. A platform, on which the villagers will build their houses, is being built out over the water.

Outside each house there was a bread oven made of baked clay (above). Fires were a common hazard in lake villages. A modern reconstruction of one of these villages on Lake Constance burnt down some years ago. The most famous lake village in England was at Glastonbury.

At the same time, in order to feed all these people, cultivated fields and pastures had to be extended and the woods were cut back even further. The farmers began to mark the edges of their fields, and jealously guarded their boundaries. A far cry from the days of rambling villages with unlimited land there for the taking!

Conflicts between the tribes multiplied. Metals were used to make swords rather than ploughshares, and herdsmen and peasants for whom a stick was once an adequate defence went armed with swords and lances of iron – to use against each other.

In the sixth century B.C. this settlement on Biskupin island in Poland started to expand. A small town with parallel streets of terraced wooden houses was built. A broad road overlooked by high ramparts made of oak beams and earth went all round the town. Spiked poles provided a lethal barrier in the moat.

The fort of Dun Aengus in the Aran Islands was protected by
a remarkable forest of large, irregularly-shaped stones,
presumably put there to slow down attacking invaders.
They look remarkably like modern tank traps.

An attack on a fortified village or 'crannog' at
Craggaunowen in Ireland. The British attackers have better

weapons and armour. This is in the Iron Age, close to the
beginning of history.

BURYING

THE DEAD

For fifty thousand years primitive men buried their dead in caves, or not at all. From about 4000 B.C. they began to construct artificial burial chambers like caves. These megalithic monuments – megalith means 'big stone' – were built with blocks of stone that often weighed 20 to 40 tonnes. The earliest builders used large stones which they found lying around; but their successors soon learned to detach large blocks from the bedrock. To make it easier to haul them on rollers to their destination, they cut mortises or notches in these blocks into which ropes or wooden tenons with ropes attached would fit and grip the rock. The stone's surface was smoothed with a mallet afterwards. Sometimes instead of mortises they left knobs (tenons) projecting from opposite sides of the rock, to which they could attach hauling ropes.

The funeral of a chief: the grave, dug in heavy clay, is being plastered with red ochre, perhaps to preserve either the dead man's body or his spirit. His valuable seashell necklace and his weapons are buried with him.

TOMBS AND MENHIRS

There were two kinds of tomb: in one kind a passage led to a burial chamber (or several chambers), and in the other kind the dead were buried along the side of the passage itself. Originally these tombs were covered in earth or in smaller stones, making large mounds called barrows or tumuli, but in many cases the soil has now been eroded, leaving the stones exposed to view.

It is easy to imagine this funeral ceremony (right) at the long covered gallery at West Kennet barrow in Wiltshire. This type of tomb could hold the bodies of more than 100 people.

A huge tumulus, as big as a natural hill, is being built beside the sea. Workers bring up load after load of earth and rock. A foreman keeps a tally. This is the tumulus of St Michael at Carnac. The biggest such tumulus is at Silbury Hill, and is forty metres high.

This heavy block of stone is being lifted by levers. One of the men, braver perhaps than the others, slips bigger and bigger rocks under the block as it is levered higher and higher.

The standing stones that support lintels to make roofed structures are called dolmens; some stand alone and were erected simply as monuments, called menhirs.

Large, well-organized groups must have worked for years to build such monuments. The larger and more powerful the tribe, the more their chieftain was respected, and the keener his followers were to build him a worthy tomb – particularly if the chief in question was still alive!

Once the upright stones were in position (right), they were buried with a mound of earth. Then the top stone, the lintel, was hauled over timber rollers to the top of the mound, and the earth was removed. This is how Stonehenge on Salisbury Plain was built.

This menhir (above), from the Proleek dolmen near Dublin, weighs forty tonnes. It took 200 men to move it. As the megalith rolled over the round logs, the ones that came out at the back were carried around to the front again.

The chief builder controls operations by giving hand signals
and shouting commands. The task was to pull the great menhir

on to the ramp (helped by levers at the other end) and then to drop the huge stone into its ditch so that it stood upright.

MONUMENTS TO MAN

Stonehenge, the most famous megalithic stone circle of all, is a mystery: it may have been built as a temple or sacred place, but it seems also to be a kind of astronomical clock – the sun rises on the monument's axis on the morning of every summer solstice. The first stage of Stonehenge took at least thirty thousand man-hours to complete. Some of the dolmens' lintels weighed eighty-five or ninety tonnes, and were brought all the way from Wales.

The Irish tumulus of New Grange contains a long passage leading to the central burial chamber which is vaulted in 'corbelled' style. At the winter solstice, every 21 December, the sun shines right into the chamber for seventeen minutes, from 8.58 am to 9.15 am; like Stonehenge the New Grange tumulus tells us

A trilithon from Stonehenge. The fifty tonne upright stones (piers) have tenons on top. The lintel has holes (called mortises) carved out to fit over the tenons, so it has to be manoeuvred precisely into place.

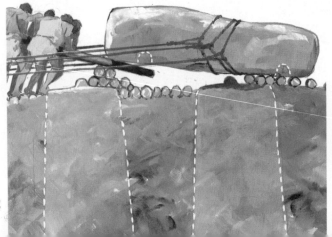

In front of the double porch of Antequera in Spain, said to be the heaviest monument in the world, the local population gathers to bury the chief and his companion.

153

At Stonehenge the sun rises at the summer solstice (the longest day of the year) along the axis of the largest three-stone arch (trilithon). At

nightfall the men will light their bonfires to burn the sacrifice.

The cairn of Barnenez in Brittany was an enormous stone structure, 85 metres long and 8 metres high. There are 10 burial chambers, 8 of which are vaulted by corbelling dry stones. Funerals like this took place there over five thousand years ago.

that these architects were also for some reason interested in astronomy. New Grange is similar in concept to the great temple of Ramses II, carved out of a cliff at Abu Simbel in Egypt, which faces the same direction, but that was built twelve hundred years later. Another feat of prehistoric architecture is the dolmen hall at Antequera in Spain. It is 24 metres long, 6.5 metres wide and 3.3 metres high; the entire building is made of only 31 enormous stones, weighing up to 320 tonnes each (1600 tonnes in all). Even this, however, is dwarfed by prehistoric man's largest monument of all, Silbury Hill, covering 2.1 hectares and rising 40 metres above the surrounding countryside.

How to cut a block of stone. First, chisel a line of holes, then hammer in wooden wedges. When they are soaked in water the wedges swell up and split the rock.

Index

159